Unf*ck Your Feelings

A Roadmap To A Happier Self

By Maria Colomy

Contents

Chapter 1. What's going on?

In the 90s grunge rock helped us all discover our inner teenage rebel, and while none of the bands of the day sang any songs with this title, the mantra of "Fuck your feelings" and "fuck anything that causes me discomfort" became the norm.

We carried our tough exteriors into adulthood, and while we removed the piercings and the band tees and traded them for adult clothes and adult jobs, and often kids, marriages, and families the residue of ignoring and minimizing feelings has landed us exactly where we don't want to be: kind of fucked.

So while cramming an emotion down into your pocket like an old tissue may often work in the moment, the exact same thing will happen. If you keep stuffing and keep stuffing eventually the trash is going to overflow.

You can take it to another can, and then to a dump truck, and then to the dump, if that's really your desire – but just like the dump – the trash may be out of sight but it's still there, and some day, someone's going to have to clean up the mess.

How often are we told to ignore what we feel, even if it happens by way of masking? Boys growing up are told, tough boys don't cry. Women are especially told not to be angry, difficult, and are often prone to people pleasing. We each carry our own set of societal programming whether we choose to or not. We've been exposed to social programming from our very birth, when we exit the womb into a congratulatory "It's a girl/boy!" which comes with its own set of unspoken expectations: Be straight, go to school, have a career, get married, have kids, retire – oh and while you're at it – you should also change the world, be great, never fail, take responsibility, contribute, participate, etc.

While I do believe that there does exist a 'right' amount of pressure, one that helps us thrive and not settle for our own comfort, I keep hoping to find the balance between the external expectations and the internal ones, because a desire for a perceived 'more' is really just our natural need for novelty and newness.

As much as we need routine and safety, humans also require a balance of novelty and newness in order to keep life interesting. We are not meant to become stagnant, and while some religions traditions say that desire creates all suffering, desire is a natural human state.

We all have a natural desire to fit in, to be loved and accepted, to do as well as we want to do, and to feel safe in our own skin. What we do not have is a natural desire to do things like: sit in a classroom for 8 hours a day when our bodies are designed for movement and play. Similarly, working 40 hours a week when we only take of 2 days sounds like insanity when you put it on paper.

Some people really thrive in this routine for periods of time, and maybe some do for their whole lives, but there is a good portion of the population who wants either more or less for their lives – and both of those things are a net positive. Less can absolutely be more if freedom is what makes you thrive, while more can be more if that is what lights you up.

One of the quickest paths to unfucking your feelings is to be true to yourself, while also finding a balanced way to respect those in your life who depend on you – because, let's be honest, not everyone can pack up their lives or walk away or move to a new city tomorrow.

When I suggest being true to yourself what I mean is: putting your oxygen mask on first before you give to others. What would it mean to wake up a little bit earlier, or stay up a little bit later to create time for yourself? This could be time for exercise, writing, working on a side hustle that you've always dreamed about, meditation, reading, or whatever thing that you keep making excuses for.

I should say here that I do have the benefit of a deliberately child-free life. I am also blessed to have healthy parents, and my own health, as well as a great, and sometimes bumpy career. I may be writing from a perspective of relative freedom.

Prior to that though, there were five years that I was absolutely not free: marriage - and when I arrived at the point of "enough" I'd abandoned myself, over and over, for five years. I was a miserable mess. I was 100 pounds overweight. I had a miserable job, my relationship was miserable, and I had spent the previous 4 years trying to save my marriage, as it circled the drain.

I've always found books that change me, and at this time I could not even tell you the name of the book – so to whatever author helped me back then, I'm sorry that I can't give you credit. I decided that I wanted to lose weight, and had just began working at a job I really loved, around some healthy people who enjoyed uplifting others. I was not used to this type of support but it was wonderful.

Pretty soon, I was waking up 2 hours before work to go to the gym, and to meal prep, and within 9 months of dedicated diet and exercise I'd lost 95 pounds – as one friend put it – that's an entire human being – even if it's a small one. That's a huge accomplishment. It was, and even now I tend to minimize it.

My point in sharing that story is – even when I really felt trapped I eventually became sick of my own crap. I became so sick of it that I was willing to do whatever it took to get out. Even then, I was fighting for my peace, I just didn't know it yet.

I am now 47, and that weight loss was over 20 years ago.

Now that I've been on this path of change for over 20 years I feel like I have almost enough experience to write about it, but only because I buried myself in research until I discovered something that both felt true, and was easily applied to my life in reality, with real results.

Even in looking back on my weight loss journey, seeing how my mindset changed as I got physically stronger and ate healthier reminds me of the importance of addressing things physically, mentally and spiritually – because even now, I go through phases of not applying what I know, and then paying the price.

In spirituality we are told, you just need to feel the feeling all the way through, and eventually it will run out. In religion we are told, give it to god, you don't need to worry about it – just 'let it go' – because that's so simple.

Don't get me wrong, a lot of these ideas can work for a range of situations. An example would be, deciding not to give a fuck about what others think – or more accurately, what you think they think – because more often than not peoples' actions are about themselves, and not about us.

A hypervigilant mind can decide that everyone and everything is out to get us. Truthfully, until I understood the science and psychology behind this I was positive that I was a Highly Sensitive Person. I can read the room and tell you the exact moment I said something that you didn't like.

I can feel the moment someone discards me energetically, sometimes weeks or months before they decide to tell me. I heard some of my more 'woo' friends describe themselves as being "an empath" which these folks believe is different than merely having empathy – the supposed empath believes that they are sensing what others feel, think, etc.

Maybe they are – but what I do know is that once I had the lens of understanding trauma I could clearly see how I'd spiritualized my own hypervigilance.

Honestly, saying that I am a Highly Sensitive Person or an empath, or even calling oneself intuitive is so much more romantic than saying "I've experienced trauma, my nervous system is different."

When someone says the t-word where does your mind go? "You're not missing any limbs..." right? Did your parents die in a plane crash? Were you abandoned, in a fire? Did you go to war?

As I write this in the year 2023, I'm secretly wishing there were another word – because even in the research, they've started saying "big T" and "little t" which feels even more inadequate.

Discovery

What is trauma, really? Well, first I want to say this, while I truly love and respect the research and the researchers, and those I have learned from over the past several years, could we please, for the love of god and all of humanity figure out a way to label this in a way that people don't cringe?

The word 'trauma' feels like it's as loaded as the word 'religion.' The preconceived notions we have about the t-word have already been demonstrated when I asked the question "when someone says trauma where does your mind go?"

In one of my most difficult relationships the other party had horrible PTSD from going to Iraq and probably from a number of other things that we never discovered. At the time I was absolutely not trauma-informed, I was trauma-blind.

I remember him having a degree of vanity about his appearance and one day when he was deep in his trauma, he said to me... one of the hardest things about looking well is that people don't believe you when you say you're not well.

This is the double-edged sword of pretty privilege. You might get jobs easily, and you might attract friends, partners, and social support easily – but try to get a doctor to see you as ill. I remember deliberately never wearing makeup to the doctor's office because I already knew that if I didn't "look sick" I was going to be told I was lying.

Then once that happened, I would have the cognitive dissonance of wondering if it really was just in my head, followed by the infuriating feeling of knowing that it wasn't.

When someone outside of our own physical body tries to dictate the experience, we are having it can be extremely confusing. Already we tend to hand our sovereignty over to the guy 'in the white coat' without questioning things – at least a good portion of the population, anyways.

As a person with a gift for pattern recognition, for me, learning then experiencing is how I learn, and also how I have formed my beliefs. You can tell me that it's true but until I can apply it and show myself that it's true it doesn't fully integrate.

I can seem to be a bit of a know-it-all because of this trait – but frankly we should all feel responsible to one another when it comes to discovering truth. There is truth everywhere if we are willing to see it, and the truth of trauma hit me, first like a ton of bricks, but later – more like the relief of a cool glass of water. A truth that actually felt true. A truth that made my physical body relax and allowed my mind to see the pattern with so much more clarity, discernment, grace and forgiveness of it.

Finally, this was a feeling I could both own, and allow to not be my fault – or anyone else's. That is the gift of truth. It just allows you to see from a much higher branch on the tree. The larger your perception can expand the more most things make sense – especially if you thrive on pattern recognition – which, not to spoil it for you, might also be one of the gifts of trauma.

Acceptance

When we live in a world of duality everything is good or bad, and we toss everything into one bucket because someone decided the goodness or badness of every little experience. Then, the more we learn we realize that a lot of this doesn't make sense to the body, and especially depending on the level of religious doctrine involved some of the trauma we experience begins to come from the self.

Self-loathing, disgust and self-hatred are the source of so much ugliness in the world. When we hate the self it can be a very simple step to hate everything about everyone else, too. This is truly the essence of duality. Everyone is an "other" instead of seeing reality for what it really is – you are another me – I am another you, and we are all just trying to get through this strange maze of "culture" and reality with our minds and hearts intact.

So what if we could lean into "it just is" instead of "is it good or bad?" Having a feeling does not make you a bad person, even doing a bad thing does not make you a bad person. We all do hundreds of dumb things over the course of a lifetime, because frankly a lot of cultural ideologies that we adopt, are pretty fucking dumb.

The desire for a constant stream of goodness is truly fucking you over. I'm sorry, and I'm sure there's a nicer way to say this but truly, the desire for nothing but goodness and the belief that avoiding any discomfort of any kind is healthy is quite frankly just insanely unhealthy (in my not-always-humble opinion).

Joy is our birthright – so is gratitude, laughter, peace and all of the other wonderful things you can think of. Unfortunately, you don't get there by running toward goodness and pretending that nothing else exists.

Honestly, I am not even sure that I could've ever arrived at those places without really diving into the other end of the pool – and while perhaps I didn't want to go into the darkness, a time came when I realized that there's nothing wrong with the darkness. We plant seeds underground before they sprout – and after they do sprout what do they deal with? The harsh, hot sun, wind and weather – everything else.

The darkness is where we grow. The darkness is where we're protected – because honestly to see the rest of the picture can also be pretty dark.

Here is the warning: once you learn what I'm about to share you can not unsee it. Like me, your new set of lenses will color everything you see, and you will wonder why a trauma-informed world doesn't exist. You might look at your former states of 'wokeness' and laugh a little bit, at what you thought you knew – because this new lens is like the decoder ring you wished for as a child.

This new lens unlocks so many mysteries that you, too, can become an obnoxious know-it-all, and you too can decide when it's appropriate to share, and when it's best to just keep it to yourself and observe. All I ask is that you use your new superpowers wisely – first for yourself, and then to help others when you can, and only when asked.

Not everyone wants to talk about their t-word. Not everyone wants to admit they have the t-word and an even far greater many might toss this book out the window before getting to chapter 2 – because the t-word is for people who are the p-word.... Right?

Integration

So now that you have some base information there's an exercise you can do – depending on how your life has gone you may need a spreadsheet or an online timeline tool. On the following page is a list of things that your body can and may have perceived as a traumatic event.

See if you can create a trauma timeline for yourself as a way to document a new perspective. This is not to create a victim mentality – it is to create an honest self-inventory. The purpose is not to do further harm, but to show you that in reality, you have been through a very normal human experience that also involves trauma.

Many therapists like to differentiate between a "Big T" Trauma and a "little t" trauma – but the reality is that your body doesn't really care if it's a big "T" or a little "t" and your opinion about the size of the trauma should really be taken off the table, for this exercise. You're documenting.

It's okay if you end up overwhelmed partway through, and need to come back to the exercise. It could take you an hour, a few days, or a few weeks.

There is no deadline or timeline on your healing, and you really should go as slowly or quickly as feels good.

There can be times that revisiting your trauma puts you into a light trauma response. I have a great piece of work that I've written that everyone wants me to publish. When I go back to read it or try to edit the work I end up feeling exhausted for several days, and I don't want to go back to it immediately. I would love to publish it someday but since I am still in the healing process, it still holds a charge for me.

While doing this work it's good to remember that healing is not linear, and much like breathing it is not something we get to be done with. Life will continue to happen, things will stress you out, and if you're reading a book like this hopefully your own self-reflection will continually lead you back to 'Why am I reacting so strongly? How can I chill the f*ck out?'

This is why having a clear map, and then learning to identify how your body is responding to things is useful. You don't need to spend a ton of time in the memories of trauma – as a matter of fact, unless you are working with a professional regularly, I would not suggest that as a means of finding your way through.

Typically, the time to do that is when you can discuss such things and they do not dysregulate you. It feels important to differentiate between creating a timeline, and deeply revisiting past memories. The goal of this work is to help you become more regulated, and not to dysregulate you further.

For me, the helpful part of this exercise that quite often I minimize what has really happened. I mask and I hear my anxiety saying that it wasn't that bad, and that others had it worse. While that may be true – trauma is not a contest, and you're not here to win.

Trauma is a pattern in the nervous system, and we're here to address the mechanics of it so that we can all feel just a little bit more joy.

Was your nervous system exposed to:

✓ Traumatic birth
✓ Trauma during your mom's pregnancy of any kind – including violence in the home, poverty, danger, longterm distress like uncertainty or fear.
✓ Childhood surgeries, prolonged illness
✓ Isolation or neglect
✓ Sexual abuse of any kind

- ✓ Physical violence of any kind
- ✓ Being terrorized with religious beliefs
- ✓ Being terrorized with anything that creates prolonged fear.
- ✓ Poverty
- ✓ Bullying, harassment, being socially outcast
- ✓ Spankings or other physical means of discipline (regardless of the intent or intensity)
- ✓ Intentional physical abuse or violence
- ✓ Witnessing abuse or violence
- ✓ Natural disasters, acts of "god"
- ✓ Car accident
- ✓ Dental trauma
- ✓ Surgery
- ✓ Loss of a loved one
- ✓ Loss of your social support system even if through an innocent event like a move.
- ✓ Having an addicted, unavailable or immature parent. This might also include other caregivers or family members – anyone close enough to influence our lives.
- ✓ Unstable home environment, even if something seemingly common like having an angry parent who explodes, but not all the time.

I feel like I could write 10 more pages, but hopefully I've created a clear picture of what we're looking for – we're not always looking for intent. Yes, often our parents spanked us to teach us some lesson or with the perception that the lesson was keeping us safe in the future – for now, remove intentions from how you think about traumatic events. I'll say it again – your nervous system isn't interested in your opinion – whatever scared you, scared you.

As the youngest of four, the "baby" I was always the first target for being picked on by the entire group. I remember having a particular fear of beetles and spiders as a kid. One summer we were at the park. Wyoming is really windy, and on this particular day my hair had not been put up so it started to tangle with the wind.

It was probably a leaf or something quite innocent but one moment I thought I had a bug in my hair, and within minutes, I'm crying and red-faced. All of my siblings were screaming, laughing, "There are so many bugs in your hair! They're all over you! GET THEM OUT" and of course I'm maybe 7 years old – terrified, screaming for help "Noooooooo!!!!!! GET THEM OUT!!!!"

Do you think there was a single bug in my hair? Do you think my body gives a fuck when we discuss that memory? Even now, at age 47 there's a little nervous pit in my stomach just thinking about it. The fear that my body felt was so real – and no, that one isn't on my timeline but maybe it should be.

Trauma is what your body thinks it is – if you spent nights afraid of what was under the bed, maybe include that – but also if you had siblings who bullied you, and parents who never stepped in as adults to stop it – include that. Social support systems are one of the most powerful things we have as social creatures. The social co-regulation we receive when someone puts their arms around us and tells us that it's okay is so enormous that my body reacted as I typed that.

Yes, I'm sorry to say but we all need hugs. That's a real thing too – and it's one of the best ways to unfuck your feelings. Literally within seconds oxytocin, our bonding hormone floods the body and feelings of safety and okayness wash over us.

Have you ever heard of a Thunder Shirt for dogs? It's essentially a compression garment that mimics the pressure of a hug. If you are in a trauma response and don't have a person around for a real hug, you can put your shoulders into a corner, pressing backwards with your arms around yourself to give yourself a squeeze and the sensation of a hug.

Whoever designed the straightjacket may have had this in mind – however... being forcefully restrained may have the opposite effect. I just go back to this one question: what would a trauma-informed world look like?

Maybe a hug instead of a straight jacket? Maybe a hug instead of a slap across the face? Maybe a hug instead of isolation and shame? Just maybe.

Identifying Emotions

A few years back a popular mantra popped up in the spirituality world, "There are only two emotions, love and fear." While I appreciate this oversimplification as one that can help us to decide on duality (ie good or bad) I don't find it useful in addressing my trauma.

This is all to say that we experience an array of emotions regardless of if we can name them or not. Somatically, which just means "in the body" we can experience emotion without words. If I ask you to bring up when you lost your dog or your kitty – or your grandma – there are words that show up in your mind: sadness, grief, longing, loss – but there's also a physical sensation in your body that is there without the words.

What does an emotion feel like in the body?

- ✓ Hot or tense behind your eyes
- ✓ A heaviness around the heart
- ✓ Like you might vomit
- ✓ Heat or tension in the low back
- ✓ Your chest might explode.
- ✓ Butterflies

✓ Sweaty palms, pits or other parts.

✓ Tight shoulders

✓ Heaviness in the shoulders

✓ A lump in your throat

✓ Like you want to pound your fists, shake your leg, kick, run, or flail around like a child having a tantrum.

✓ A desire to scream, punch, or run away.

✓ A need to cover your eyes or face (reduce sensory input)

This is an introduction to somatics. Quite often the experience of the body scan instead of using emotion words can be enough to create the body to sigh, yawn, or simply relax into a state of ease.

Truthfully, I do not find duality useful in most things, but especially not in healing. Do you know what the original sin was in the bible? It had nothing to do with women or temptation. It was the discovery of duality, which is false. In the Christian bible story, they "ate from the tree of knowledge of good and evil."

Duality is simply a belief that some things are evil and some things are godly, when really life just IS. Creation created all things – not just the things we find pleasant. Demons are not making all the bad decisions in the world for us – unless you want to call trauma the demon that it is.

Eternity is not something held for a select few who chose the right religion out of the 4,200 possible options. God is not nefariously waiting for you to ask for the wrong thing so he can do the WWF smackdown on you. There is no devil in the details – and really do you think that you need to 'be careful what you wish for?' Is our creator really an asshole the way a human would be, or is that just humans personifying everything the same way we do our house pets?

It has already been scientifically proven that our consciousness survives physical death of the body. Eternity is already guaranteed, my friends, you don't have to earn it, you don't have to want it, and you get it even if you didn't ask for it. Study the afterlife for a week and you'll forget everything you thought about it. Nobody's soul is burning in hell for having sex or committing suicide. Pleasure is not a sin and it never was. It can be a great way to regulate the body, though.

Creating self-hatred through religious beliefs is terribly traumatic – this is not 'god' speaking, I can assure you of that.

Regardless of if you believe in a creator or not – consciousness is real and it survives the body. This requires no religious commitment on your part. I spent a lifetime obsessed with the afterlife in my hopes to have dropped dead by now. I'll have to explain this awkward trauma response later, in the section about trauma responses – and yes, the belief of dying at a young age is one that broke my heart as I learned this information.

Restoring Feelings Of Safety

Neuroception: When the nervous system keeps the score. First, this is not to downplay the amazing work of the book The Body Keeps The Score. In fact, the wisdom of that book began to lay the groundwork for work like this – just steps beyond that simple fact, and taking the additional components of not just understanding the system and its automatic response, but also how to play with that automatic response, in order to downregulate back to safety.

Neuroception is the body and nervous system working in tandem with the environment, and external social queues to inform you of one thing: is it safe or not?

If it's not safe, we begin to feel the very normal symptoms of a fight, flight, freeze or fawn response. These behaviors might be annoying to those around us, but they are literally how the body reacts, quite on its own. It might look like:

- Frozen or flat response.
- Inability to think of what to say in the moment.
- Feeling the heart rate, and blood pressure rise sharply. Shallow breath, sweating, numbness in the hands or face.
- Irritability, moodiness, inability to have fun or feel joy.
- A feeling of "GET ME OUT OF HERE NOW!!!!!"
- Rage
- People pleasing, being complaint, attempts to keep the peace
- Self-blame, toxic self-shame, denial that the other party does not feel safe to your nervous system

I want to reiterate that these reactions are normal, and expected responses when the body senses trauma.

Even more annoying – if we get stuck in a fight or flight response it can look even more dramatic:

- Neck, shoulders, and upper back that feel stuck or frozen, or like we're bracing for impact all the time.
- Skin or digestive issues
- Symptoms that are in parallel to fibromyalgia, Hashimoto's, and other 'mystery' illnesses.
- Food, chemical and environmental sensitivities.
- Brain fog
- Body aches, sore all the time for no apparent reason.
- Hair loss, psoriasis, eczema.

As a matter of fact, the studies around Adverse Childhood Experiences show that those with a score of 2 or higher are more likely to experience even serious health conditions like diabetes, high blood pressure, heart disease, etc.

Trauma is real whether you like the label or not, and even more importantly – trauma is whatever your body thinks it is! Your brain doesn't even have to agree – and your opinion about it won't change anything.

This is why stuffing it down, burying it and hoping it will die off by itself is useless. You might as well have dumped a pound of fertilizer on those seeds because now they've grown – and quite frankly they're thriving. Ignoring trauma is gas on the fire.

As humans, we love conformation bias and we love believing our own crap. I think that's why it took me 20 years to get to this information. For so so long I called my trauma everything that it was not.

I called it my 'addictive personality' and I called it codependency. I called it insecurity. I called it fear (not love!) – because spirituality told me there were only two emotions and I decided that was correct. I don't want to minimize addiction or codependency – because trauma IS those things – but those are the symptoms of ignoring it, of not looking it right in the eye and saying out loud "I see you, there you are."

This is the only way that I have found to get the monsters out from underneath the bed. The only way is to get a flashlight, shine it brightly, only to discover there's just a bunch of dust and cobwebs down there. There is no monster, there is no victim. We're just a bunch of unchecked nervous systems responding to one another – that is, until we're not!

This is why early on I said that once you see and learn this information you cannot unsee it – you see it everywhere. You see it in a police officer abusing a victim, and screaming at them for "changing their story" when really what happened was, when their nervous system calmed down, more information came through.

What would a trauma informed world look like? One where wellness and healthcare were in line with one another, and one where we did not get punished for simply feeling what we feel.

Chapter 2. Now What?

Now that you have a basic understanding of this, what can you do?

Mental

This is going to be a process, and it may not happen overnight – and hey – maybe it will! Sometimes we hear a new phrase or see a new idea and suddenly our entire framework shifts.

During the mentalization and processing of this new information you might have a tendency to feel removed from it, as if you're dissecting the emotional web created in a film.

Putting distance between you and the trauma is a great step to take, but first we really do need to truly feel whatever repressed emotions may have settled into our bodies and memories. This is some of the heavier lifting in the healing process, but also the most rewarding.

By understanding trauma, our history with it we can better understand those who came before us, and even how or why things may have occurred.

This is not to make excuses for those who hurt is. It is not to invalidate what happened – and even if we look back and have a hard time believing that 'they did the best they could' we can at the very least see that everyone is carrying their own story, their own past, their own pain and their own challenges.

Nobody is getting a free pass, and even those whose lives appear somehow better, easier, more fulfilling – even those people are living lives we know nothing about. This might be a great opportunity to practice focusing on the self, rather than making assumptions about others.

Wrapping your mind around the reality of your past might involve talking with a trusted friend, a good therapist, a coach, or taking the time to write and process internally, rather than externally.

During this time, it can be good to remember that we should not rely on a single person for all of the emotional support that we need. Quite often the person who is your best friend may not be the best or most qualified person for the job.

Taking the time to identify who is in your life and what role they might play can also be extremely valuable. Decide what you will share, when you will share it, and with whom you will share.

Also, as you navigate the mental processing and your social support system you may realize that not everyone is up for the job.

Transforming emotionally will change your life. Period. As you become more aligned with your true self the relationships around you may also change, and some of them may even cease to exist.

For me, this was one of the most difficult parts of my healing journey. During the time that I did the most meaningful personal self-development work I also lost many of my important relationships, including a best friend that I had for nearly a decade.

I don't want to minimize the truth here. The relationships that were unable to sustain my growth had their problems before the growth. However, after I chose to take drastic responsibility for everything and everyone in my life my boundaries changed. What I was willing to tolerate changed. Even though I approached these conversations with care and reverence there was no way for me to determine what the receiving party would do when I decided to set a boundary.

With boundaries, quite often it can take several tries, and multiple conversations – but sometimes the other party may be entirely unwilling to negotiate the terms of the relationship.

I don't want to suggest that every single person in your life will abandon us as we grow, but I do want to be real here – some people will be uncomfortable with this new version of you. We have to allow them the discomfort.

There will also be friends and relatives who cheer you on, and who love seeing you make progress. There are people who will stand by you, who will understand that your desire to do and be better is not a threat, but an asset.

They say a rising tide lifts all boats, but the reality is that some of the boats topple over if the change happens too quickly.

Decide ahead of time that you are okay with how things might go, and remember most importantly – you only need to share what you feel you need to share. This applies all the time, when it comes to your personal, internal life. You get to decide how and what to share – and you also get to decide when privacy feels safer.

Unfucking your feelings is about ownership and responsibility – not making it about how someone else might react, or what they may think of you.

You're not doing this for them, and regardless of how enmeshed your relationships may or may not be – doing things selfishly does benefit those around us. We've all heard the concept of putting our own oxygen mask on before we try to help others. Instead of seeing it as selfish, we might recontextualize this as personal responsibility – because truly, that's what it is. It's merely a way of saying, "I'm choosing better so that I can be a better person in your life, too." What a gift!

Physical

Supporting the body physically is absolutely necessary while doing this work. This may look like an added layer of personal responsibility that you weren't really looking to take on, but the reality is that our physical body can only support us if we support it.

Doing simple things like drinking enough water and taking a few walks a week may seem oversimplified or even unnecessary but, ignoring these things is akin to ignoring the oil light in your car.

The car might drive for a few more days, weeks – or even months before it decides to completely implode due to your neglect. In contrast, simply keeping up with the regular maintenance of your vehicle can make it last years longer. Just think about the difference between taking care of something you love and enjoying versus simply keeping something you love but never doing anything to maintain it.

Think about the contrast you feel between the two scenarios I just described – and even the regret that you might feel when you realize, "I could've handled this differently,"

Future you needs you to show up now. Future you needs you to stop ignoring the maintenance.

The best time to plant a tree was 20 years ago, and the second-best time to plant a tree is today. Start now – so that future you is prepared, and so that future you is someone whose life you want to be living in.

Regret is one of the biggest mistakes we can make. It points back to the triggering statement "they did the best they could with what they had," because, really – did we?

I don't want this step to be a punishment or deprivation. I am merely asking you to see the importance of creating an environment in the body that supports your effort.

There's no reason that we all need to be Olympic athletes, and for those who are – go you! There's also no reason that we all can't get outside for a walk a few times a week or swap out our sodas for water. How much or how little you do is up to you, but please do not ignore this important piece of the puzzle. If you want the car to operate, it needs gas and oil – and if you want it to really shine, it's going to require just a tiny bit more effort.

Just like the environment in your body is important in this process so is your physical environment. I don't just mean your home, I also mean your car, your workplace and any places you're spending time. Granted, you will not be able to make changes in every single place, however, this is another great opportunity for a personal inventory.

Do you enjoy being in your home? Do you love walking in the door? Do you enjoy where you sleep?

There's been a fascinating and humorous trend going around on social media lately where men complain about the size of a woman's TV – and women retort by making fun of men who have a massive television and no bed frame or sofa.

Are you proud of your living space? Does it have everything a great living space needs? Is it, at the very least, mostly clean and organized?

Your environment around you is both a reflection of your inner life and a support system for your outer life. If you've ever taken a stab at feng shui, the Chinese art of organizing the home energetically – you may have experienced the power of your environment.

I am not suggesting you create a new enemy to conquer (your environment), but simply recognize that your life, as a whole, needs to support you. This is not about having the highest thread-count sheets or making your home look like Martha Stewart redecorated for you. This is about finding the net positives and the net negatives and making adjustments.

Ask yourself one thing, "How does it make me feel?" then, make adjustments from there. If you're coming up blank – "It's just a house/apartment, etc." how would it feel to create some gratitude around the situation? What do you like about it and why did you choose it? Was it 'all you could find at the time' or was it something you really wanted? Are you living in a situation that makes you feel disempowered or small in some way? Too many roommates, or living with your parents when you're way too old?

What adjustments are you willing to make? If you're not willing to make any adjustments physically, then mentally what adjustments could you make?

Could you be more grateful? Could you be more organized? Could you appreciate the location, or cost, or something about the experience? Is it temporary? Are you excited or afraid about what comes after this?

Some of the ways you might support your body while getting your emotions in order could look like:

- Daily movement
- Reducing or eliminating sugar
- Reducing or eliminating caffeine or other stimulants that might be increasing cortisol
- Reducing or eliminating processed foods from the diet
- Taking supplements that support your nervous system

Emotional

Sometimes you need to just let it out – really you always do, but by now you know that. There's an old saying that the only way out is through. Feeling the depth of your sadness, at times, is needed to process it.

Some of the more emotionally-centered techniques might include writing and journaling. You could consider finding a trauma-informed therapist or coach to talk with.

Emotional processing is also a great opportunity for social co-regulation: talking with a close friend or family member who understands you might be a great way to reflect. It's not always best to heal in a bubble of your own opinions, but there's also nothing wrong with productive self-reflection.

Chapter 3. Don't Trip!

Discovering potential pitfalls and hangups as you discover a new way of life.

First and foremost, the healing journey is non-linear, and it is common to have a ton of progress, and then for the pace to change. Another healthy thing that may occur is that you may realize that you do not need to be constantly 'working on yourself,' and sometimes it's wonderful to just enjoy life!

Allowing joy is a form of self-work, because turning off the rumination about trauma, even intellectualizing it can be just another bucket of crabs – and the goal here is – no more buckets and especially no more crabs.

Spiritual Bypassing

For years this was my go-to because it was all I knew. For decades it was, "I chose this. I must've needed this lesson," and so many other phrases like asking myself why I chose these people as my teachers.

The spiritual narrative first led me to become very codependent. Once that happened the next phase was the codependent/narcissist or empath/narcissist narrative which, albeit true in many many ways – is just another bucket of crabs. I say this because it creates a victim perpetrator narrative of "what they did," when in reality we also participated in various ways.

We participated by staying, and by attempting to change someone who never asked us to change them, and who likely is not ready for change.

We justified this behavior by believing that if only they would have done something different – or had things returned to the honeymoon phase before they discarded us things would've been wonderful.

The reality is that things were never wonderful and you were hoodwinked. Rather than accept this you tried to change the person and the situation – and you called yourself loyal, caring, concerned, and a bunch of other things that were not true, in order to make your codependent behavior acceptable.

I did this. I did. I saw myself doing it and I promptly admitted it, but until someone pointed it out I just could not see it.

I had injected my know-it-all-ness into the situation because I had decided to believe that I could read into another person's situation. Have you caught yourself doing this? You are just so positive that you know what's best for someone else that you inject your advice and opinions where nobody asked for it?

I have ruined relationships this way. I didn't always know that I was doing it, but afterwards I did have to look closely at the situation to see where I was at fault. This is doing the work. This is unfucking your feelings. It is not to place blame on yourself, or on the other party – but really to see how you may have contributed, and how you might adjust in the future.

You might also reflect on ways to forgive yourself so that you don't create a secondary shame shit storm. This is not necessary – shame spirals are easy for us to fall into, and even the self-talk that comes with this behavior can be somewhat automatic. How many times a day do we think things like, "I am such an idiot!"

Are you, really? Because it looks like you're reading a book and taking the time to learn about yourself. You've probably accomplished dozens and dozens of

things, and somehow you've gotten through life –
right? The inner self-talk that we carry needs to be
looked at and recognized for what it is, and so does
the spiritual gaslighting.

You did not choose to be in an abusive situation.
Quite often, even if we are not codependent, being in
an abusive situation can bring out these traits. There
are many high-achieving individuals who have high
empathy, high agreeableness, and other traits that
often make them susceptible to toxic environments.
My suggestion is to avoid blame narratives altogether
whenever possible, and this includes blaming god, and
blaming the devil.

Find accountability wherever you can. Learning
your truth is the most important thing for your
nervous system, but also realizing when you are
believing something that isn't true like "I'm such an
idiot," is part of this truth. You know that is not true.
Most of us made the best decision that we could at the
time – and once we knew better we did better, even if it
took some time.

This journey requires grace and forgiveness,
especially for yourself. You deserve grace. You are

already forgiven – so forgive yourself. There is no angry, judgmental, narcissistic god. There is only compassion and grace – you've had a tough road – and your nervous system is just asking for some grace.

Intellectualizing

Another of my favorite bypasses is intellectually bypassing. It can be really easy to learn about trauma, have a few 'ah-ha!' moments, and then attempt to move on.

The greater reality about trauma is that it wants to be seen and heard, and felt and then released. What I mean by this is that there is a layer of knowing that something did happen, plus the layer of writing it, sharing it, talking through it internally if that is the only safe space, but it needs to be known. Once it is known (seen and heard) you do actually need to feel whatever you feel about it.

Grief can come up in realizing how trauma kept you from going after certain dreams or goals, and grief consists of some very uncomfortable phases – including denial, acceptance, bargaining, depression, and anger. These are normal parts of grieving.

You might be grieving the relationships that were affected, and there might be deep, and very justifiable sadness in processing what you've been through.

This is another space to allow things, but to not get too stuck in them. The process of writing things out, talking to a trusted friend or therapist can be really helpful. Remember that if you do talk to a friend, be careful that you're not asking them to carry something that they may or may not be equipped to carry.

When you decide that you are ready to process things, just be sure you are in a safe place to do so – and if you do decide to choose a therapist, I would highly suggest you find a trauma-informed therapist who has been trained recently enough to understand the somatic and nervous system processes that are associated with trauma. More in the section below labelled 'I Hate Therapy."

I Can Do Everything Alone

Oh I can too! You should see my self-help book collection, it is amazing! Before that it was every spiritual book you could imagine, by every guru you could imagine, but I bet you already knew that! From quantum physics to every type of yoga and meditation and mantra an essential oil – every biohack and every organic vegan grocery item you could imagine – all wonderful luxuries that I am enormously grateful for having access to – they did not heal the trauma.

You can listen to every podcast, and you can self-isolate and bottle it up, but one reality that I found in this work is that I needed community – not the appearance of community like subscribing to a podcast or scrolling TikTok – but really having people to talk to when I needed to talk. Safe people who were educated enough to level with me in the reality of my traumatized nervous system. People who were safe enough to sit in discomfort with me when I lost my shit, or needed to cry – or needed to rage or vent about something that had gone awry.

Don't do this work alone. You could but why would you want to? Sometimes just hearing someone say, "You shouldn't have had to go through that, I'm sorry, I bet that was really hard," can feel like the warm hug that it is.

You are a social creature wired for connection and love. Your traumatic memories of people might be telling you that people are not safe, but let's be more accurate here – abusive people are not safe. Safe relationships do exist, and you do deserve to have them.

Our nervous systems do require social regulation. Sitting with another human being can be so healing. Laughing, reflecting, and just holding space for one another can be one of the best ways to heal. Remember, safe relationships DO exist, and you do deserve to have them.

Group therapy like Codependents Anonymous, www.coda.org, can be a great non-religious way to find some social co-regulation, even if you go to the meeting and don't share – just hearing the stories of others, and being in community can be quite healing.

Find ways to work your way out of the belief system that you cannot rely on anyone, and that people are a source of pain. Equally, it can be a great time to remember that all people cannot be all things to us – if you have a great friend don't wear them down with carrying everything with you. Find ways to have a support system, a whole one. You deserve that.

I Hate Therapy

Years ago I had an experience with compound grief-two of my close people had died very suddenly and a third longtime friend attempted suicide, shooting off half of his face and missing his brain entirely. I began to spiral. The two friends had just been there the pervious week, and then they were gone, just like that. At this time in my life I had already lost dozens of people, and death was not something new at all. However, with a compound grief it's as if you never get the chance to gain your footing – life knocks you down three or four times and before you know it you're unrecognizable, even to yourself.

We've all seen it happen – the guy who loses his job and then his wife and then his kids – or the woman who loses her lover, then her parents, then her career – compound grief can really kick you to the ground. It's earthshattering – and it can leave you in a state of shock, or not wanting to be here. It can look like rage, irritation, the inability to control your emotions – a feeling like you can't take anymore.

My first time seeking therapy for my Complex PTSD I was in a state of compound grief. At the time I had a corporate job with insurance and was able to use insurance for therapy, so naturally this was the route I went. If nobody ever told you – when choosing a therapist it's best to ask for a referral – from a human being. Even one who used that therapist might be logical.

Anyhow, I browsed the list of names and locations online, mainly choosing one that I could get to easily after work, and that was in the neighborhood. I wish I could remember this woman's name, but I suppose it may not bode well in the long run. It's better that I don't remember her name.

In the first session she wanted my trauma history – verbally – I became so dysregulated that I could hardly speak, and I sobbed uncontrollably for the next six hours. I am not even sure how I drove home.

By the second visit she had diagnosed me, wanted to medicate me, and by the third visit she was yelling at me for buying a book about the diagnosis she gave me. I don't know how many times she was late making her tea, or doing some other task – and when I took my training at Arizona Trauma Institute I realized how dysregulating even this behavior can be for someone dealing with trauma.

It literally felt like she was not present, and it barely felt like she gave a fuck. Unfortunately, since I did not have a stick to measure her against I just assumed this was what therapy was going to be like. I absolutely hated it.

Several months later I had my first experience with a somatic therapist. This experience was a few steps better than the previous one, but it was still really missing something for me.

As things progressed in my life I found myself in a very toxic situation that had further retraumatized my already-sensitive nervous system. I decided to take courses at Arizona Trauma Institute so that I could educate myself on how to even vet my own therapist – this seemed like the best way to reverse engineer the problem—learn from the people who train the trauma informed.

This experience all by itself is what empowered me to write my books. Finally, something made sense in such a way that my entire body was able to relax in its presence.

We've over applied diagnosis and underapplied care. When you're traumatized, even the diagnosis can be retraumatizing and suddenly you're having an ADHD research session with WebMD and Reddit forums. It can be hard to know who to believe, and who to trust. Ultimately it has to be you, trusting yourself, and knowing when you feel the truth, but working with a trained professional can be really wonderful.

There was a time where I never would've used those two words in the same sentence, but trauma-informed therapy is different than traditional Cognitive Behavioral Therapy in that it focuses on an individual's strengths rather than deficits. It helps you see where you've been thriving, and how your responses were just how you chose to get through a tough situation.

With trauma-informed care you won't be digging up what's wrong with you, but instead, what is right. It's a completely different approach, and in my experience

I had much more encouraging result. I didn't think that I could enjoy or look forward to therapy.

Some mental health care can feel like it's just slapping the sunburn. Trauma-informed care is just the opposite, and attempts to soothe instead of further irritate.

Unhealthy Relationships

There are hours upon hours of content on the internet about the narcissistic relationship dance. The scripted way they behave, and the scripted way that you behave back. You could spend years consuming endless narc content about how they lie and the stories they tell.

The reality is, you can also get stuck in an endless loop of blame. Identifying the pattern is useful but only to a point. Because the point of identifying the pattern is to stop the behavior. Ideally, you would no longer put any energy toward anything that didn't help you evolve or grow in some way. The relationships that sucked you dry would no longer exist.

The greater reality is, people are people. You are going to have to deal with those who are kind and honest, and those who are not. The best use of the lesson from "those" relationships is using the information to identify toxic patterns in the future. Once you do identify this, because it will cross your path again, your job is to observe.

First, observe their actions and behaviors without jumping to conclusions or diagnosing anyone. See if you pick up on the nuances of the relationship. Are they cheering you on for personal gain or because they actually believe in you?

What happens when you don't feed into the energy? It does take two to tango, so if you don't dance does the energy change? Can you feel more aware of the potential manipulation before it occurs? Do you feel mentally and socially equipped to do the dance again? If not, you have permission to step out.

Holy Effing Religion

When I was a kid, I thought, how cool that a group of people believed so much in the freedom of belief that they came to this new land, literally FOR religious freedom. How idealistic and patriotic. How wrong, how wrong I was.

The more I learn the more unbelievable this world is. The old saying that truth is stranger than fiction still rings true. As a child of the mid-seventies I truly believed in idealism, feminism, equality, and justice. My naive little heart jumps at the thought of peace on earth.

The only perspective I can share in this section is the one that I have. I am not going to study even more religions to give you a deeper dive, because just like my first two books, most often we can identify qualities to look for, without knowing or understanding the nuances of each flavor.

Fundamentalism, fuck me. This particular brainwashing package is deeply disturbing to me. I consume far too many documentaries which will allow me to generalize, but we should start with some facts.

The United States does not protect children from adult predators when using the guise of religion. In all but two states there is no age limit for how young a female can be married. This means that without her consent, since she is not old enough to give consent, a girl, yes a girl (under 18) can be married with only the permission of her parents.

So often close family members or friends abuse children, and then that child, undeveloped brain and all, is forced into marriage. Even more often the victims of these situations do not know their rights, nor do they have anyone to advocate for them. In most states, a woman can not even go to a domestic violence shelter if she is under the age of 18.

Women are still property, even in our blessed land of the free. Please do not underestimate what you just read. This means that a child, even an infant, under the guise of religious union can be legally married.

It's almost painful to think that in the year 2024, with all of our advancement in technology, mental health, intelligence, this is still where we are. This is still what we do. This is still who we are. This culture is a cult.

Submission is next on the list. In all types of spiritual fuckery we are told to that to submit is the holiest of options. Unfortunately, the prevalence of using god to gaslight rears its ugly head once again. We can call "gods will" just about anything we want to. The reality is, religion is not mental health, and it is absolutely NOT a trauma-informed approach. If anything, religion seeks to blame everything on either demons or god's will – leaving no room for the actual human to have its own God-given right: free will.

Spare the rod, spoil the child. Spankings. Physical violence. Let's just call it what it is. Spanking is violence. It is using physical harm and domination to control behavior, or to punish behavior that already occurred. It's also pure insanity.

Having an adult three times your size wail on you to get its way, usually smacking some joy out of you along the way, is literally insane. Who thought this would work? Parenting and discipline should absolutely be rendered, and children should be taught right from wrong. However, typically what adults see as "bad behavior" is more often nervous system dysregulation. It's unresolved fear, it's trauma, or attention seeking, or some type of struggle that a child may not have the words for.

Sometimes its mere childhood curiosity or "I thought it would be fun!" behavior – and really, truly, how is this "bad"? Testing rules and boundaries is appropriate behavior for a child. It's as appropriate as curiosity and fun.

I once heard the question asked that, "If all mammals get the zoomies why don't humans get the zoomies?" and the sad but true punchline was that, "It had been beaten out of us as children."

Let that sink in. Piousness is not our natural state. Uptight. Stick up your ass. Whatever you decide to call it -- can you imagine how much easier our lives would be if we didn't feel so entitled to our disgust with "others" and how they do life?

Oddly the stick-up-your-ass part of the population are also the folks forcing children to marry adult men. Is there a triple-edged sword? I am just not seeing the benefit.

Your Nervous System

Your nervous system has a language all its own, and once you learn this 'second language' managing and navigating your moods and emotions will just be a matter of noticing and choosing an activity to up or downregulate the nervous system.

Your nervous system has two modes: sympathetic=fight or flight, and parasympathetic or "rest & digest". Both states have other qualities besides the two listed. Sympathetic might include: fight, fight, freeze, fawn (people pleasing) and parasympathetic will also include the state we get into while exercising or going for a walk in nature.

If you think of a toddler pitching a fit or a chihuahua screaming at the neighbor, your nervous system is pretty much the same. But, unlike the toddler and the chihuahua your brain has a bunch of programming that's been added like: sit still, be polite, stop complaining, wipe those tears off your face. I'd like you to put those on ignore, for now.

Think of a kid waiting impatiently without someone shouting at them to 'BE STILL!' and they're likely swaying, looking around, moving and fidgeting or talking to a friend if they're around people in their age group.

Managing your nervous system is almost that easy. Try to start listening to your body -

- When do you feel like you need to run away?
- When do you feel like you need to scream?
- When do you feel like pushing or kicking?

- When does your leg start to bounce, when do you fidget?

What about the emotional triggers?

- Upwelling of emotion with a strong sense of fight or flight.
- Need to talk to them RIGHT NOW and tell them EVERYTHING I've ever needed to say(please, don't!)
- Sweaty arm pits or hands.
- Rageful or strong angry feelings like... how dare they or... I can't believe this!
- Core might feel hot or intense.
- Shutting down, feeling completely numb. Not caring about anything.

It's important to understand that the nervous system is like a cup. Once its full it just overflows and when you try to put more in it has no-where to go. This is the 'shut down' or numb state that you may have experienced at times. You're just done. This often happens if we're experiencing grief or depression, or if multiple things have gone wrong at once.

Allow yourself to experience the state of alarm, as well. Something did happen, and no matter how big or small your nervous system wants to respond, so let it. When an animal is chased by a predator in nature it will run (flight) or freeze. Once it comes out of this state there is often shaking or trembling, or sometimes just a head shake.

The exercises in that follow will mimic what our nervous systems naturally need to do to process emotions, and instead of focusing on how you feel emotionally (sad, hurt, scared, etc.) we will focus on a conversation with the body.

Chapter 4. Let's Do This.

Applying what we've learned.

Self-Regulation Techniques

Think about a toddler having a tantrum on the floor and what is happening in their body. Even the pounding of the fists, the kicking and lashing out of the body are signs of a nervous system releasing built up energy.

In Emotional Freedom Technique or EFT tapping the 'karate chop' portion of the hand is the same part of the hand that's getting stimulated if we use a punching bag - or, if we were a toddler, when we throw a tantrum.

The tantrum is a discharge of emotion and energy, and quite often once its over there's a crash - just like the barking chihuahua taking a nap after it's fit of rage.

Self-regulation techniques are a form of self-help that can be used to regulate one's mood, thoughts, and behaviors by releasing energy in the physical body. They may include physical activity, mediation, and breath work.

In this section we will cover different self-regulation techniques to help you regulate your mood. These are listed in no particular order. You should choose the ones you enjoy so that they are easy to employ when you become overwhelmed. Right brain versus left brain: The right brain imagines, and the left is logical and protective.

Choose A Left-Brain Task

Quite often when we are fantasizing about our grievances, also known as rumination, we're in right brain mode. If you can switch to a left-brain task, you can often slow down the racing thoughts. Sometimes earthly things like paying a few bills, doing some laundry or dishes can help to calm the nervous system. If you've ever known someone who cleans out of anger you've seen this. The physical activity is a release of the energy. The angry cleaner may not know it, but they're also self-regulating.

The logic of a left-brain-oriented task can help push us back into a hippocampal-dominant mode, taking us out of fight or flight, which helps to distract us from our angry thoughts. Another common technique is bilateral movement and exercise. This is the act of moving both arms and legs in order to stimulate the vagus nerve which helps regulate your mood by releasing serotonin and dopamine - two natural chemicals in our brains that are associated with happiness, relaxation, calm and contentment. Think taking a walk, dancing, jogging, drumming, swimming, etc.

Vagus Nerve Stimulation

Another technique is vagus nerve stimulation. It works by stimulating the vagus nerve which helps regulate your mood by releasing serotonin and dopamine - two natural chemicals in our brains that are associated with happiness.

Here's a quick example of a Vagus Nerve Reset that you can experience in just a few seconds:

30-Second Vagus Nerve Reset

1. Tap the side or 'karate chop' area of your hand while doing the following:

2. With your eyeballs (not your head) look into the far RIGHT corner of your eyes. While doing this, count by increments of 12 up to 60.

3. With your eyeballs, look into the far LEFT corner of your eyes. While doing this, hum the tune of a song for several seconds. You might notice a hard yawn or a big sigh. You've successfully stimulated your vagus nerve.

I created this method myself based on years of using EFT tapping, which is another great way to stimulate the vagus nerve. You can look this technique up online and learn it in about 5 minutes. It's similar to the above but you'll find different combinations and areas to tap, and many involve an affirmation that says "Even though I am feeling

_____ I completely love and accept myself."

With any and all of these options the key is to make them comfortable and enjoyable. If a mantra or affirmation feels cheesy to you, you're not going to do it, so don't use that method. If you hate going to the gym, but don't mind going for a walk, choose a walk. Regulation strategies are only going to become habits if they work, and if you enjoy them. My goal here is to give you many options, so that you have an arsenal at your fingertips when you need them.

Exercise

All exercise has positive impacts on our mental health, but beyond that, movement helps to move and discharge energy, but especially simple walking, especially outside can be a wonderful regulation tool.

Meditation

One of the most commonly suggested self-regulation techniques is meditation. Meditation involves focusing your attention on the breath, body sensations, and sounds in order to help regulate one's mood. You can also choose to do a mental task that helps you focus on something else. An example would be doing 100 breaths with three seconds of being very present before moving on to the next number. The old method of counting sheep or imagining blackness to fall asleep is a simple form of meditation.

Meditative Hobbies

Some people find hobbies like knitting to be a wonderful meditative practice. Meditation does not have to be spiritual, it does not require a mantra or even closed eyes. Meditation is the process of slowing down the mind and thinking. Have you ever wondered why men love fishing? Do you think they know they're meditating?

Getting out into nature is one of the most enjoyable ways to self-regulate. There are dozens of popular mediation apps that can also help you find your favorite way to mediate.

One reason mediation is so commonly suggested is that it does assist in rewiring the brain. The connections that help us relax become stronger. In 6-8 weeks you become stronger at reacting to stress in a healthy way.

Many people find it patronizing when someone says "go take a walk" or "have you tried meditation?" These suggestions are not meant to be patronizing - as you can see here there's a reason they're common regulation strategies.

Water & Immersion Therapy

Immersion therapy like hand washing, swimming, baths, and cold plunging can assist in nervous system regulation. The restorative effects of water on your nervous system can help to boost your mood and improve your sleep. The negative ions in water help attract positive ions to the body, also increasing mood. Maintaining proper hydration and using electrolytes in the body are an excellent way to help regulate the nervous system and our mood.

Even a cold splash of water to the face or immersing a hand or arm to cold water can be enough to trigger the response. Essentially your body sends its energy to recover from the cold. When cold water shocks your body, your brain produces norepinephrine, a neurotransmitter and hormone, which helps you gain better focus and attention, and also improves mood.

Norepinephrine also plays a role in regulating your emotions. Try 30 seconds of cold water at the end of your shower to see how you feel over the next several hours.

There's a reason cold plunging has become so popular in the past several years - it works!

Shaking & Vibration

Next, there's shaking. Have you ever noticed how a raging chihuahua will be so angry that it shakes from head to toe? Afterwards, the dog will 'shake it off' by doing a little head shake and often go sleep for a few hours.

This is a proper response to stress, and part of the reason animals do not hold onto trauma as often as humans do. An animal naturally 'shakes it off' and then goes to rest. We can't always do this in human life.

Using a vibration platform, or exercises that make your muscles voluntarily shake can replicate the 'shaking it off' behavior. Even stomping your feet on the ground can be a good way to reground if you are in an environment where that's appropriate (maybe not in your meeting?). It's important not to fall into the trap of 'shaking off' your emotions through negative behavior, such as overeating sugary foods or drinking.

Dancing

Dance is also an excellent self-regulation activity. While exercise is great, dance incorporates FUN, which we quite often forget to have when we're dealing with stress, which is likely if you're reading this book. In addition, singing is a great way to stimulate the vagus nerve. EFT stands for Emotional Freedom Technique. EFT tapping is another common vagus nerve stimulation exercise. You can google or hop on YouTube to learn EFT tapping in under 5 minutes.

Hugging/Compression

Putting the hands over the heart, hugging, and deep breathing are all great ways to lower your heart rate and vagal tone. The vagus nerve is a major nerve that runs from the brain to the body cavity and right through the heart. Its branches run through the middle of each ear in what is called the "vagus" or "sinu" nerve, connecting with structures in each side of the neck-the internal jugular vein (located on both sides) and carotid artery (on one side).

There are entire books dedicated to toning the vagus nerve, and it's great to learn as many as you can so you can find ones you enjoy.

Safe Social Connection

Next, there's social connection. Truly nothing helps more than to feel safe with a trusted friend or loved one who just gets you. In the COVID era many have been socially isolated and may even associate fear with socialization.

Don't forget - there's FaceTime and Zoom - and reconnecting through real phone calls is important. We are social creatures meant for connection. If you can't see and hug your friends, having a pet is a great way to achieve regulation. Pets can calm us down by simply being there for us or by providing physical contact. They offer emotional support, teach responsibility and they're just plain fun! They may also mimic our need for social and physical connection. It's nearly impossible to be crabby all day if you have the joy of a pet. They really are little angels on earth.

Sex & Orgasm

Sex with a safe partner, if that's an option can be a great way to regulate and connect. Safe sex and other pleasurable activities like massage and touch can be great options IF sex and physical touch feel safe to you. If they don't, you should avoid this strategy for self-regulation, however, even giving yourself an orgasm is a great way to regulate the body and reduce cortisol.

Orgasms release chemicals like serotonin, dopamine, oxytocin, and vasopressin. Tantric sexuality can be a great way to harness the power of these chemicals. If you don't have shame issues around sex and the body, orgasms are a wonderful built-in self-regulation tool.

Long Slow Breathing

Your next built-in self-regulation tool: Long, slow deep breaths. They can calm the nervous system within seconds, especially an extra-long exhale. This is a signal to the body that you are safe.

Stretching

Self-regulation through stretching can be a wonderful practice. Stretching is not only a great way to improve your physical health, but it also provides many mental benefits. It can decrease stress, boost energy levels, increase blood flow, and release endorphins. Stretching has been proven to be an effective treatment for anxiety and depression. You can use long slow exhales in combination with stretching to deepen the stretch and to help get more grounded in the body.

Simple Somatic Reset

Sometimes even stopping to breathe, feeling your bottom in the seat and your feet on the floor can be enough to bring us back to a regulated state. Some people find it helpful to focus on their breathing during times of high stress. Learn some conscious deep breathing exercises from yoga or qigong and practice them often.

Prayer, Mala Beads, Spiritual Practice

Another strategy for regulation is prayer. If you're spiritual or religious, prayer can be a wonderful tool for self-regulation, as well as silent reflection, the repetition of a mantra, or the use of prayer/mala beads or a rosary. The repetition of the beads in the hands used as a way of counting, this method can be very relaxing since one does not have to count or keep track consciously. Journaling, and especially gratitude journaling is another option similar to prayer. Prayer is not always asking for favors from a higher power, often it is being grateful for our lives and those around us.

Laughter

Now, onto one of my favorite and less serious methods of regulation, laughter. When was the last time you laughed - HARD - until your face or ribs were hurting? Laughter, even forced laughter, can be a great practice for getting your body to relax.

Quite often we're severely lacking joy and fun in our lives, especially with the reduced social interaction we've experienced since COVID. Find a favorite comedy station, satire website, or default to cat and dog videos if needed. Anything that will induce a deep belly laugh will do, but if you can socialize and laugh in person, even better. We are, after all, social creatures wired for connection and support.

Skin Sensations

Physical sensations like skin brushing with the palms are another way to help reassociate with the body. Similar to immersion therapy, just relocating body sensations can help to regulate the body, depending on your past and your preferences.

Punching, Kicking, Intense Exercise

Especially for anger release, punching and kicking exercises are a great way to stay active and release excess energy. Starting with the basic punches and kicks, you can work your way up to more advanced techniques such as sparring or mixed martial arts training.

Quite often with trauma we have a natural response to push things away, and this physical release can be a perfect way to do that.

Avoiding 24/7 Screens

Fun fact: sitting in front of a screen all day has been shown to increase Complex PTSD and Trauma Responses, or a dysregulated nervous system. Sometimes just getting outside for a walk can help.

Start thinking about what your body naturally wants to do. It wants to relax, it wants fun, joy, pleasure, and safety. The body knows what to do - we've just evolved so much language around what it means to be at rest and not constantly chasing work, experiences, or busy-ness.

We were not meant to work and run full force 24 hours out of the day. Regulating the nervous system requires you to put self-care first, and to begin being honest about when your body is giving off alarm bells.

Doing the work.

So what if it's not "work" at all? Can you still participate? To begin, try to start a routine of allowing yourself to feel, release, repeat.

Next, allow some allowing. Being in the mode of forcing yourself to heal all the time is not what we're going for. In a sense it's the opposite of that, with a bit more knowledge and whatever level of routine you enjoy, but none of it should feel forceful or stressful.

Start feeling into your days. Especially women have hormonal swings that may leave us feeling up and energized, or zapped and not-so-energized. Both states are okay, and having the space to lean into a low energy day the same way we lean into the high-energy ones was one of the biggest breakthroughs I've ever had.

Remove the laziness narrative and allow your nervous system to be in whatever state it needs to be in. You don't always need to stimulate or caffinate yourself into forced action if that's not what feels good.

That's not to say that taking an energizing walk isn't a wonderful addition to any day – just realize that a state change is wonderful, and allowing can be equally wonderful. Try just letting go a bit more. What will eventually happen is that your higher energy days will form into what I call flow-state days – days where I can produce 2-3x the work in a few hours than I could if I were trying to force it out of myself. Just allowing this flow of highs and lows with less judgement allows my nervous system to relax and release. Your body just wants to be heard.

Having Fun

I yearn for the days of being a silly kid with no agenda and far fewer rules built up in my mind about what is or is not allowed. Think of all of the programming that you've been exposed to. Are any of these automatic for you:

- Sit still.
- Don't embarrass me.
- Don't make a scene.
- Don't be such a brat.
- Keep quiet.

Quite often we had parameters around when we were and were not allowed to be our full selves. Even more often those rules had to do with how we might make another person 'appear.' In reality, nobody probably gave a crap – and if they did they likely don't remember, now.

Who exactly are we people-pleasing for? Do you have an invisible audience judging you? What does it sound like? Seriously, let's unfuck that little fantasy. There's no audience – and if there is one on the other side – they're probably wishing you'd dance and play a lot more often. Truly – there's no audience, and quite often we make up the meanest, nastiest one that could possibly exist. *Choose the other one* – the one whose got your back, is cheering you on, and knows well and good that you are allowed to feel well and good.

Joy

Finding the line between toxic positivity and allowing is the goal here. I'm not asking you to force joy, or to chase feeling great 100% of every moment of every day. What I am suggesting is that if you look, there's already an overlay of joy that exists that we often fail to recognize.

Were your needs met today? Do you have more food than you could ever possibly eat in your home? Do you have more clothes than you could possibly wear in your home? Do you have abundance, financial, physical, or otherwise that you've failed to recognize?

It can be common to think we did it all ourselves but did we really? Somebody hired us, bought our product, invested in us, guided us. Someone approved the loan, someone gave us the chance we needed, when we needed it. Lean into the goodness that exists and you won't have to force joy. All of your needs have been exceedingly met. Say it out loud.

Let's Clear Some Shit Up

What about the energy of overabundance? Do you have closets that could be cleaned out or items that you could give away? Somebody probably needs the excess that you have. You could sell it but are you ever going to get around to doing that? Are you really going to make 12 trips to the post office?

Find a local group online and list your items for free or a very low cost and allow people to enjoy what you're not using.

Make way for new energy to come into your life by removing what no longer serves you. I hate to admit that one of my favorite ways to motivate a good declutter is to watch an episode of any of the popular hoarding shows. Not that another person's misery is entertaining, but seeing them get through it and come to the other side is inspiring.

Realizing that there may be fear of poverty, or grief or loss behind the reasons we keep things can be very eye-opening. Why do we need to keep a bunch of clothes that we never wear, and then still buy more?

You can blame this on consumerism if you'd like to, but what I am asking about here is you, personally. What are YOUR reasons for doing this behavior? Hint: 'consumerism' is not the answer we're looking for. You already know it in your heart and in your gut. It's whispering to you "What if I run out? What if I can never buy that again and I need it someday?"

Let all of that go. You know that it is not even a little bit true. Life has given you upgrade after upgrade and you still fail to realize that more upgrades are ahead. This does not always mean bigger, better and more expensive – it means that the quality of our lives continue to improve so long as we are participating in life.

Sometimes this means richer relationships, finding meaningful ways to give or serve, finding ways to share your gifts and talents with the world, or directly with others. Life was never meant to be lived in a bubble.

Chapter 5. Celebrating YOU!

Holy shit! You've worked hard. Have some fun! What are some healthy ways that you could give back to yourself? Investing in yourself might look like radical self-acceptance and self-love.

It might look like physical care, good food, sunshine, clean water, movement, connection. It might look like not overspending, not overindulging to escape, not escaping. It might look like creating a life you don't want to escape from. Create some goals, and then routines that lead to your new goal.

Take a course, explore new ideas you've been wanting to explore. Talk to someone who is doing what you wish you were doing – remember not to live your life in a bubble. A tree produces fruit not for itself, but for the environment around it.

You are the only expert at you – and you have a uniqueness that nobody else has. The world wants you to show up as you, without masking – without asking for permission, without making yourself small.

Conclusion

You've got this – you don't need me to tell you what to do. You're invited to go live your amazing life.

About The Author

Maria is a life-long learner who shares from her personal experiences of trauma, drama, humor and hilarity. Having lived most of her life refusing therapy, and then later falling in love with it, she looks back with a new, even funnier lens and shares her experiences of healing, laughing, and rediscovering joy.